HOW GOD SUPPLIES OUR NEEDS

How To Access The Unlimited Supply of God for All Your Needs

FRANCIS JONAH

IMPORTANT

My name is Francis Jonah. I believe all things are possible. It is because of this belief that I have achieved so much in life. This belief extends to all. I believe every human being is equipped to succeed in every circumstance, regardless of the circumstance.

I know the only gap that exists between you and what you need to achieve or overcome is knowledge.

People are destroyed for lack of knowledge.

It is for this reason that I write short practical books that are so simple, people begin to experience immediate results as evidenced by the many testimonies I receive on a daily basis for my various books.

This book is no exception. You will obtain results because of it.

Visit my website for powerful articles and materials

www.francisjonah.com

FREE GIFTS

Just to say Thank You for downloading my book, I'd like to give you these books for free.

Download these 4 powerful books today for free and give yourself a great future.

Click Here to Download

Your testimonies will abound. Click Here to see my other books. They have produced many testimonies and I want your testimony to be one too.

Counselling Or Prayer

Send me an email if you need prayer or counsel or you have a question.

Better still if you want to make my acquaintance

My email is drfrancisjonah@gmail.com

Other books by Francis Jonah

3 Day Fasting Challenge: How to receive manifestation of answers

How to Have Outrageous Financial Abundance In No Time:Biblical Principles For Immediate And Overwhelming Financial Success

5 Bible Promises, Prayers and Decrees That Will Give You The Best Year Ever: A book for Shaping Every Year Successfully plus devotional (Book Of Promises 1)

Influencing The Unseen Realm: How to Influence The Spirit Realm for Victory in The Physical Realm(Spiritual Success Books)

Prayer That Works: Taking Responsibility For Answered Prayer

Healing The Sick In Five Minutes: How Anyone Can Heal Any Sickness

The Financial Miracle Prayer

The Best Secret To Answered Prayer

The Believer's Authority(Authority Of The Believer,Power And Authority Of The Believer)

The Healing Miracle Prayer

I Shall Not Die: Secrets To Long Life And Overcoming The Fear of Death

Three Straightforward Steps To Outrageous Financial Abundance: Personal Finance (Finance Made Easy Book 1)

Prayers For Financial Miracles: And 3 Ways To Receive Answers Quickly

Book: 3 Point Blueprint For Building Strong Faith: Spiritual:Religious:Christian:Motivational

How To Stop Sinning Effortlessly

The Power Of Faith-Filled Words

All Sin Is Paid For: An Eye Opening Book

Be Happy Now:No More Depression

The Ultimate Christian: How To Win In Every Life Situation: A book full of Revelations

Books:How To Be Free From Sicknesses And Diseases(Divine Health): Divine Health Scriptures

Multiply Your Personal Income In Less Than 30 Days

Ultimate Method To Memorize The Bible Quickly: (How To Learn Scripture Memorization)

Overcoming Emotional Abuse

Passing Exams The Easy Way: 90% and above in exams (Learning Simplified)

Books:Goal Setting For Those In A Hurry To Achieve Fast

Do Something Lest You Do Nothing

Financial Freedom:My Personal Blue-Print Made Easy For Men And Women

Why Men Go To Hell

Budgeting Tools And How My Budget Makes Me More Money

How To Raise Capital In 72 Hours: Quickly and Effectively Raise Capital Easily in Unconventional Ways (Finance Made Easy)

How To Love Unconditionally

Financial Independence: The Simple Path I Used To Wealth

Finding Happiness: The Story Of John Miller: A Christian Fiction

Finance Made Easy (2 Book Series)

Click here to see my author page

Contents

INTRODUCTION 15

CHAPTER ONE 20

CHAPTER TWO 26

CHAPTER THREE 32

CHAPTER FOUR 39

CHAPTER FIVE 45

CHAPTER SIX 51

CHAPTER SEVEN 58

CHAPTER EIGHT 63

CHAPTER NINE 72

INTRODUCTION

Jesus was emphatic when he told us to ask for our daily bread from God. This means that he envisaged God supplying our daily needs:

Give us this day our daily bread.

Matthew 6:11

That is what fathers do and God is our heavenly father as believers. It is the reason why we look to Him to perform His responsibility of fatherhood to us. One of the greatest responsibilities of fatherhood being the supply of the needs of children.

We are the children of God. This is why Jesus asked us to refer to the Almighty God as our father:

After this manner therefore pray ye: Our Father which art in heaven, Hallowed be thy name.

Matthew 6:9

Since our father is supposed to supply our needs and we know we have a father who is more than able to supply our needs, it is necessary to know how God supplies the needs of His children.

This is because many are frustrated since they still cannot access the provision of God for their lives.

This book is written because there are ways to access the supply of God and when knowledge of these ways are absent, the children of God tend to suffer for nothing.

After all, it is clearly the lack of knowledge that causes the children of God to perish:

My people are destroyed for lack of knowledge: because thou hast rejected knowledge, I will also reject thee, that thou shalt be no priest to me: seeing thou hast forgotten the law of thy God, I will also forget thy children.

Hosea 4:6

Take the bird for instance, the Bible says that God feeds the birds of the air, which is true. You will agree with me however, that God does not put the food into their mouths directly.

There is a mechanism by which they access the food God provides them.

Behold the fowls of the air: for they sow not, neither do they reap, nor gather into barns; yet your heavenly Father feedeth them. Are ye not much better than they?

Matthew 6:26

We are much better than the birds of the air but surely, God will not put the supply in our mouths.

The birds that God feeds go round and find the food that He has provided for them amongst other things.

This is the reason by the leadings of the Holy Spirit, I have discovered several ways God supplies the needs of His children.

By going through this entire book diligently, you will come to the place where you will recognize and enjoy the supply of God for your life.

Let us delve into the beautiful revelation of God's word that will take us to our next level.

CHAPTER ONE

LIMITLESS SUPPLY

The supply of God for our needs is without limit. This means that there is no need that God cannot meet and exceed in our lives. Think about it and let it sink deep down into your mind and spirit.

The scriptures make this point forcefully:

Now unto him that is able to do exceeding abundantly above all that we ask or think, according to the power that worketh in us,

Ephesians 3:20

This is to tell us that God's supply far exceeds every need we can have or imagine. This is a glorious revelation.

Never for a second think that God cannot supply that current need of yours. His supply is more than enough.

Did you know that the earth and all that is in it belongs to God. Anyone who possesses anything here is just a custodian of what belongs to God.

The earth is the LORD'S, and the fulness thereof; the world, and they that dwell therein

Psalm 24:1

If all things belong to God, it means He can meet your needs and more. My God. This is powerful. We serve a living God and even the devil knows the capabilities of our Almighty God.

When He wanted to make sure we understood His limitless power and ability to supply beyond our imagination, He introduced Himself in a peculiar way:

Behold, I am the LORD, the God of all flesh: is there any thing too hard for me?

Jeremiah 32:27

There is nothing too hard for God Almighty. No need he cannot meet.

He is the God of all flesh. If certain men have reached the place where they are able to meet 100 percent of the needs of the people they are responsible for, how much more the creator of the heavens and the earth?

God supplies according to his riches

One important thing that we must take note of is where God supplies from.

Paul one day showed us where the supplies of God come from and it is certainly grand:

But my God shall supply all your need according to his riches in glory by Christ Jesus.

Philippians 4:19

The great thing we discover in this scripture is that God supplies our needs according to His riches in glory.

God is rich. He supplies our needs from His riches. His riches are inexhaustible. They can meet our needs a million times over and there will still be far more than what was disbursed.

Peter had a taste of this supply and was overwhelmed:

Luk 5:3 And he entered into one of the ships, which was Simon's, and prayed him that he would thrust out a little from the land. And he sat down, and taught the people out of the ship.

Luk 5:4 Now when he had left speaking, he said unto Simon, Launch out into the deep, and let down your nets for a draught.

Luk 5:5 And Simon answering said unto him, Master, we have toiled all the night, and have taken nothing: nevertheless at thy word I will let down the net.

Luk 5:6 And when they had this done, they inclosed a great multitude of fishes: and their net brake.

Luk 5:7 And they beckoned unto their partners, which were in the other ship, that they should come and help them. And they came, and filled both the ships, so that they began to sink.

Luke 5:3-7

Peter had caught nothing after working all night. When Jesus came onto the scene, he caught so much that he beckoned another boat to come and even after the second boat came, they both began to sink because of the weight of the supply.

That is the kind of supply you will receive after you finish and implement the truths in this book.

Let us delve deeper into the desire of God to supply your needs.

CHAPTER TWO

GOD WANTS TO MEET YOUR NEEDS AND HAS MET THEM

If you have ever wondered if God is interested in meeting your needs this chapter will settle that issue once and for all.

Beyond that, you will realize that God has actually supplied your needs and is waiting for you to take advantage of it.

God did not spare His best because of you

God has already given you the best that He had. As a result there is nothing else He cannot give to you.

This is seen vividly in the book of Romans:

He that spared not his own Son, but delivered him up for us all, how shall he not with him also freely give us all things?

Romans 8:32

God did not spare Jesus Christ because of you. His own son. His first and best. If God gave you His most priced possession, consider the things of this world that cannot be compared in anyway to Jesus Christ.

Jesus Christ is greater than silver and gold.

Jesus Christ is greater than houses.

Jesus Christ is greater than every need imaginable in this world, yet God freely gave Jesus to you.

The scripture is thus asking if God gave you Jesus, what can't He give to you. Absolutely nothing.

He can give you all things and actually, He has given you all things.

God has given you all things

God has given us all things. He did this when He gave us Jesus.

Take note of the scripture we just read again:

He that spared not his own Son, but delivered him up for us all, how shall he not with him also freely give us all things?

Romans 8:32

God with Jesus freely gives us all things. All your supply is in Christ Jesus. When God gave you Jesus, He gave you the supply to every other need.

Whether financial, health, emotional or psychological needs, He met them all in Christ Jesus.

When we delve deeper to what Paul said, you will realize the same theme playing through:

But my God shall supply all your need according to his riches in glory by Christ Jesus.

Philippians 4:19

In this verse of scripture, you see that God shall supply all our needs by Christ Jesus.

Already He did not spare Christ Jesus, He gave Him freely to us.

You have Christ Jesus and all that comes with Him. Glory to God. Your needs are supplied. You just need to take possession of them.

This concept is quite simple. When God wanted to multiply fruits, He put the ingredient for multiplication in the fruit itself, which is the seed.

In the same way, He has put our supply in Christ Jesus and given Him to us.

And God said, Let the earth bring forth grass, the herb yielding seed, and the fruit tree yielding fruit after his kind, whose seed is in itself, upon the earth: and it was so.

Genesis 1:11

The seed was in itself. Glory to God. Our supply was also placed in Christ Jesus when He was given to us.

What then limits us from enjoying this supply? We will discuss this very important subject in the next chapter.

CHAPTER THREE

THE LIMITATION OF ONE DIMENSIONAL THINKING

The fact that God supplied one persons need in one way does not mean that is the only way He supplies.

I have seen many people make some ways God supplies needs look inferior to other ways. As such, people have boxed themselves into one-dimensional thinking and this has affected them greatly in accessing the supply of God. They feel if God doesn't supply it this way then forget it.

By this pattern of thinking, they have actually limited the operation and administration of God.

It is very possible for a man to limit God in his own life:

Yea, they turned back and tempted God, and limited the Holy One of Israel.

Psalm 78:41

The Israelites limited God and it is possible for us to do so too.

I remember one day in particular when I suffered from this one-dimensional way of thinking.

I was in school and was very hungry. I had just read about God feeding the birds of the air and decided that I wanted that experience. At that time, I had exhausted my money so I waited for three days for God to supply me food to eat. I wanted God to send me the food directly through someone without a word from me. I had read of people receiving supply this way and thought this should be the way God supplies needs. Actually, they made it seem as if this was the only way they received supplies from God. Who wouldn't want that?

After three days of hunger and seeing nothing, I took my phone and called my mum. Within hours, there was a healthy sumptuous meal in front of me.

Even Jesus sometimes sent for food to eat and paid with money. His needs were not always met in one way:

(For his disciples were gone away unto the city to buy meat.)

John 4:8

Jesus could multiply food, yet food was bought for him.

Another time he asked his disciples to bring him someone's donkey:

Luk 19:30 Saying, Go ye into the village over against you; in the which at your entering ye shall find a colt tied, whereon yet never man sat: loose him, and bring him hither.

Luk 19:31 And if any man ask you, Why do ye loose him? thus shall ye say unto him, Because the Lord hath need of him.

Luk 19:32 And they that were sent went their way, and found even as he had said unto them.

Luke 19:30-32

This goes to show that you cannot limit yourself to just one way of receiving the supply of God.

It is worth noting that the ministry of Jesus kept a moneybag where the money of the ministry was kept to meet the needs they had. Judas, a kind of treasurer for Jesus at that time, held this bag:

For some of them thought, because Judas had the bag, that Jesus had said unto him, Buy those things that we have need of against the feast; or, that he should give something to the poor.

John 13:29

Although Jesus could get money out of the mouth of the fish, he still used the moneybag to meet some needs. Never be limited in how you can access the supply of God:

Mat 17:24 And when they were come to Capernaum, they that received tribute money came to Peter, and said, Doth not your master pay tribute?

Mat 17:25 He saith, Yes. And when he was come into the house, Jesus prevented him, saying, What thinkest thou, Simon? of whom do the kings of the earth take custom or tribute? of their own children, or of strangers?

Mat 17:26 Peter saith unto him, Of strangers. Jesus saith unto him, Then are the children free.

Mat 17:27 Notwithstanding, lest we should offend them, go thou to the sea, and cast an hook, and take up the fish that first cometh up; and when thou hast opened his mouth, thou shalt find a piece of money: that take, and give unto them for me and thee.

Matthew 17:24-27

Now that you have an open mind that God's supplies can be accessed through different means, let us delve into the various means we can access the supply of God.

CHAPTER FOUR

WORK

One of the ways God supplies our needs is through the agency of work.

Work is one of the most important agencies on earth and God proved so in the very beginning.

God did not allow the rains to fall on earth because there was no man to work on the land. This shows how important work is to God, to the extent that He withheld rain just because there was no worker.

Gen 2:5 And every plant of the field before it was in the earth, and every herb of the field before it grew: for the LORD God had not caused it to rain upon the earth, and there was not a man to till the ground.

Genesis 2:5

When you work, you give yourself the opportunity to receive provision from God. When you plant seeds, you get a harvest that you can eat as well as sell some to meet your needs.

When you take care of animals, they multiply to feed you and you can sell some to make money to meet other needs.

In our modern day economies, many are rewarded financially for the work they do. These financial rewards in the form of money are used by many to meet their needs.

This is why Paul encouraged that those who didn't work must not eat.

For even when we were with you, this we commanded you, that if any would not work, neither should he eat.

2 Thessalonians 3:10

Paul was very keen on this instruction because he recognized the place of work in the scheme to the supply of God for the needs of His children including the food they eat.

It is the reason He equipped us with the strength and mind to work so that our needs could be met.

The book of proverbs characteristically spoke about hard work giving you enough to meet your needs.

He becometh poor that dealeth with a slack hand: but the hand of the diligent maketh rich.

Proverbs 10:4

The scripture clearly says that if you are lazy when it comes to work, you will be poor. You will not be able to access the supply of God for your life. Without accessing the supply of God your life as well as your dependants will be miserable.

However, when you work hard, you are sure to be rich. This means that you will have more than enough to meet your needs as well as the needs of your dependants.

What a glorious mechanism by the Almighty God to meet our needs. Glory to God.

God instituted work as a means of meeting needs

There can be no dispute as to the issue of work being a means that God meets our needs.

It was one of the ways God met the needs of Abraham, Jacob, Isaac and who have you.

All these men worked and worked hard. As a result they always had their needs met by God through their work.

Work is something we must never look down on. We must embrace it fully and give it our all knowing very well that it is a mechanism God uses to meet our needs.

This is the reason God blesses the work of our hands. He knows it is a key supply mechanism that He uses. The scripture thus says:

The LORD shall open unto thee his good treasure, the heaven to give the rain unto thy land in his season, and to bless all the work of thine hand: and thou shalt lend unto many nations, and thou shalt not borrow.

Deuteronomy 28:12

God blesses the work of your hands. Recognize that and embrace work with all your heart.

Let us move on to the next way God supplies our needs.

My desire is to see your progress and prosperity and freedom from negative people and circumstances. Because of that, please permit me to introduce two courses that I believe passionately will help you.

1. To cure prayerlessness, an inconsistent prayer life and the pain of not enjoying all that God has made available to you,, click [here](#) to learn more about my [3 Day Course](#) on "How to Overcome prayerlessness" that will solve the problem of prayerlessness in your life.

2.To overcome the pain of not having enough money to live where you want, eat what you want to eat and be a blessing to the multitudes around you, I have created a *7 Day Financial Abundance Course* that will deliver financial abundance to you quickly.

Click *here* to learn more about that course.

CHAPTER FIVE

IDEAS

Another way that God supplies the needs of His children is through ideas.

Apart from working, God gives His children ideas they can use to access His supply.

These ideas come in times of prayer, worship, meditation and thinking.

When you think of the ideas that have brought the supply to many in our generation, you will see how important the mechanism of ideas is a significant means to meet your needs.

From Facebook, to KFC, to Walmart, to Tesla and what have you. All these channels of supply began with an idea.

What idea has God given to you that you have neglected?

In my book "Provision through divine ideas," you will appreciate this mechanism of supply by God.

Joseph accessed the supply of God for the whole of Egypt and beyond by an idea.

Jacob came out of poverty using an idea.

The story of a woman who had an idea that she had oil and that oil was multiplied by God to meet her needs clearly shows the power of ideas:

2Ki 4:2 And Elisha said unto her, What shall I do for thee? tell me, what hast thou in the house? And she said, Thine handmaid hath not any thing in the house, save a pot of oil.

2Ki 4:3 Then he said, Go, borrow thee vessels abroad of all thy neighbours, even empty vessels; borrow not a few.

2Ki 4:4 And when thou art come in, thou shalt shut the door upon thee and upon thy sons, and shalt pour out into all those vessels, and thou shalt set aside that which is full.

2Ki 4:5 So she went from him, and shut the door upon her and upon her sons, who brought the vessels to her; and she poured out.

2Ki 4:6 And it came to pass, when the vessels were full, that she said unto her son, Bring me yet a vessel. And he said unto her, There is not a vessel more. And the oil stayed.

2Ki 4:7 Then she came and told the man of God. And he said, Go, sell the oil, and pay thy debt, and live thou and thy children of the rest.

2 Kings 4:2-7

There is an idea in your mind right now that God is expecting you to bring out to access the limitless supply He has for you.

There is a simple process you can also use to get ideas to access the supply of God.

Simple process for getting ideas

I have a simple process for getting ideas.

I normally set my mind to work and then pray till an idea that fits my goals comes.

Step 1

I ask my mind a question

How do I access $1,000 of God's supply Or how do I make $1,000 every month?

It can be any amount depending on you.

I start small and when I accomplish it, I move higher. Therefore, you can start at $10 or $100.

Step 2

I take my notebook or journal and write as many ideas as come up. I give it at least one week. In that one week, I keep praying with my journal beside me.

Any idea that drops, I write it down.

Step 3

I select the best idea and work on it until it becomes a reality that helps me access the supply of God.

Note to quitters

Sometimes when you work on your idea, you may not get the results you want.

Go to the drawing board, learn what you need to learn and hit that idea again until it works.

Sometimes all you need to do is to learn how to make an idea work. Pray, use google, use YouTube, use amazon to get the right information that will make your idea a success.

There is already a solution that can make your idea work. Find it and use it.

From this chapter, you can easily see how God supplies our needs through ideas.

Let us move to the next way God supplies our needs.

CHAPTER SIX

PARTNERSHIP

Another way that God supplies our needs is through partnership.

When you partner with the work of God or a servant of God. You create an access way for your needs to be met.

This is what Paul told the church in the book of Philippians.

If you read the scriptures very well, you would realize that Paul was speaking to them specifically that his (Paul's) God will supply their needs according to His riches in glory.

This declaration was occasioned by their continual giving to support him and his work in the kingdom.

This has been a very peculiar way God uses to supply the needs of His children.

When you decide to partner a ministry or a servant of God, what you are doing is creating an avenue to receive the supply of the Almighty God.

Let us read the scripture in context and see what Paul was trying to tell us:

Php 4:10 But I rejoiced in the Lord greatly, that now at the last your care of me hath flourished again; wherein ye were also careful, but ye lacked opportunity.

Php 4:11 Not that I speak in respect of want: for I have learned, in whatsoever state I am, therewith to be content.

Php 4:12 I know both how to be abased, and I know how to abound: every where and in all things I am instructed both to be full and to be hungry, both to abound and to suffer need.

Php 4:13 I can do all things through Christ which strengtheneth me.

Php 4:14 Notwithstanding ye have well done, that ye did communicate with my affliction.

Php 4:15 Now ye Philippians know also, that in the beginning of the gospel, when I departed from Macedonia, no church communicated with me as concerning giving and receiving, but ye only.

Php 4:16 For even in Thessalonica ye sent once and again unto my necessity.

Php 4:17 Not because I desire a gift: but I desire fruit that may abound to your account.

Php 4:18 But I have all, and abound: I am full, having received of Epaphroditus the things which were sent from you, an odour of a sweet smell, a sacrifice acceptable, wellpleasing to God.

Php 4:19 But my God shall supply all your need according to his riches in glory by Christ Jesus.

Philippians 4:10-19

Paul was clear in communicating to the Philippians that their giving to him in partnership was to their own benefit.

It ensured that they received the supply of God. This is the reason why you must also seek to partner with the work of God as well as the servant of God.

This is clearly what happened for the poor old widow of Zarephath whose needs were met by God when she partnered with Elijah.

1Ki 17:8 And the word of the LORD came unto him, saying,

1Ki 17:9 Arise, get thee to Zarephath, which belongeth to Zidon, and dwell there: behold, I have commanded a widow woman there to sustain thee.

1Ki 17:10 So he arose and went to Zarephath. And when he came to the gate of the city, behold, the widow woman was there gathering of sticks: and he called to her, and said, Fetch me, I pray thee, a little water in a vessel, that I may drink.

1Ki 17:11 And as she was going to fetch it, he called to her, and said, Bring me, I pray thee, a morsel of bread in thine hand.

1Ki 17:12 And she said, As the LORD thy God liveth, I have not a cake, but an handful of meal in a barrel, and a little oil in a cruse: and, behold, I am gathering two sticks, that I may go in and dress it for me and my son, that we may eat it, and die.

1Ki 17:13 And Elijah said unto her, Fear not; go and do as thou hast said: but make me thereof a little cake first, and bring it unto me, and after make for thee and for thy son.

1Ki 17:14 For thus saith the LORD God of Israel, The barrel of meal shall not waste, neither shall the cruse of oil fail, until the day that the LORD sendeth rain upon the earth.

1Ki 17:15 And she went and did according to the saying of Elijah: and she, and he, and her house, did eat many days.

1Ki 17:16 And the barrel of meal wasted not, neither did the cruse of oil fail, according to the word of the LORD, which he spake by Elijah.

1 Kings 17:8-16

Because of her partnership and giving to the man of God, the needs of the widow of Zarephath were met.

It is a unique mechanism through which God supplies our needs and we must take advantage of it.

Let us move on to another way God supplies our needs. I must say that the last method is one of the best yet misunderstood ways of supply. That will come after the next way of receiving the supply of God.

CHAPTER SEVEN

PRAYER AND THE BLESSING

Another way to receive the supply of God is through prayer and the blessing.

Jesus asked us to pray for our daily bread. This clearly tells you that God can supply our needs through prayer.

When Israel needed rain, Elijah prayed and the rains came down.

God had answered the needs of Israel through prayer:

Jas 5:17 Elias was a man subject to like passions as we are, and he prayed earnestly that it might not rain: and it rained not on the earth by the space of three years and six months.

Jas 5:18 And he prayed again, and the heaven gave rain, and the earth brought forth her fruit.

James 5:17-18

God had met a need in direct answer to prayer. There are other occasions that supply to needs came directly in answer to prayer.

One that comes readily to mind is Paul and Silas when they needed deliverance. They prayed to God and praised and their need was met as a result of prayer:

Act 16:25 And at midnight Paul and Silas prayed, and sang praises unto God: and the prisoners heard them.

Act 16:26 And suddenly there was a great earthquake, so that the foundations of the prison were shaken: and immediately all the doors were opened, and every one's bands were loosed.

Acts 16:25-26

This is a clear example of God supplying a need through prayer.

This is why prayer can never be discounted as a mechanism God use to supply the needs of His children.

The Bible is clear that if we ask for bread, God would not give us stones:

Mat 7:7 Ask, and it shall be given you; seek, and ye shall find; knock, and it shall be opened unto you:

Mat 7:8 For every one that asketh receiveth; and he that seeketh findeth; and to him that knocketh it shall be opened.

Mat 7:9 Or what man is there of you, whom if his son ask bread, will he give him a stone?

Mat 7:10 Or if he ask a fish, will he give him a serpent?

Mat 7:11 If ye then, being evil, know how to give good gifts unto your children, how much more shall your Father which is in heaven give good things to them that ask him?

Matthew 7:7-11

If we ask God in prayer, He is able to supply. This is what the Bible is clearly telling us. Never hesitate to employ the mechanism of prayer to have your needs met.

The blessing comes in play when we employ it to multiply or empower what we already have to meet our needs. Jesus employed the blessing to multiply bread such that it fed thousands of people.

This is why it is important to bless your money and your food and everything that concerns you. The blessing from your mouth is powerful.

***Luk 9:16** Then he took the five loaves and the two fishes, and looking up to heaven, he blessed them, and brake, and gave to the disciples to set before the multitude.*

***Luk 9:17** And they did eat, and were all filled: and there was taken up of fragments that remained to them twelve baskets.*

Luke 9:16-17

Let us move on to the last way God supplies our needs in this book. It happens to be one of the most powerful mechanisms of supply but very misunderstood.

CHAPTER EIGHT

STEWARDS

Another way God supplies our needs is through stewards.

This is one of the most misunderstood means by which God supplies our needs. Nonetheless, it plays a major role in the supply mechanism of God.

This is the way God took care of you as a child till you grew to the point where you could take care of yourself.

In that scenario, your parents or guardians were your stewards through which God supplied your needs.

Even now, there are still certain needs you cannot meet on your own though you are an adult. God is fully aware of it and so places stewards around us at every level we find ourselves.

This concept is explained here vividly:

Gal 4:1 Now I say, That the heir, as long as he is a child, differeth nothing from a servant, though he be lord of all;

Gal 4:2 But is under tutors and governors until the time appointed of the father.

Galatians 4:1-2

As a child of God, you may still not be at the place God wants you to be to access certain things due to where you are in terms of spiritual growth.

For that reason, tutors and governors or stewards are appointed who take care of things and resources on your behalf until you come to the place of maturity.

Your main responsibility is to find out who these stewards are and ask for your supply from them.

You must understand that I am not asking you to go to them like a privileged person who is entitled to their resources.

What I am trying to say is that certain people have been placed on this earth as stewards to make sure your needs are met.

This is why there are certain pastors who can pray for you to be healed when your own prayers do not seem to have any effect. They are stewards.

This is why certain people are able to pay fees for people who could never have paid those fees on their own. They are stewards.

At any point you are in life remember these words carefully, you have a steward.

Like the birds of the air, your job is to find these stewards and they will help you meet the needs in your life.

Some people are very selfish and opportunistic. I am not talking to such people. More often than not, although that may not be the case all the time, you must have served these stewards in one capacity or the other.

Esther relied on a steward for the deliverance of the Jews:

Est 4:15 Then Esther bade them return Mordecai this answer,

Est 4:16 Go, gather together all the Jews that are present in Shushan, and fast ye for me, and neither eat nor drink three days, night or day: I also and my maidens will fast likewise; and so will I go in unto the king, which is not according to the law: and if I perish, I perish.

Esther 4:15-16

In the case of Esther and the Jews, the king was their steward who brought about their deliverance.

Esther had to ask him for his protection from Haman and his plot of death.

In the case of Nehemiah, the king was his steward:

Neh 2:2 Wherefore the king said unto me, Why is thy countenance sad, seeing thou art not sick? this is nothing else but sorrow of heart. Then I was very sore afraid,

Neh 2:3 And said unto the king, Let the king live for ever: why should not my countenance be sad, when the city, the place of my fathers' sepulchres, lieth waste, and the gates thereof are consumed with fire?

Neh 2:4 Then the king said unto me, For what dost thou make request? So I prayed to the God of heaven.

Neh 2:5 And I said unto the king, If it please the king, and if thy servant have found favour in thy sight, that thou wouldest send me unto Judah, unto the city of my fathers' sepulchres, that I may build it.

Neh 2:6 And the king said unto me, (the queen also sitting by him,) For how long shall thy journey be? and when wilt thou return? So it pleased the king to send me; and I set him a time.

Neh 2:7 Moreover I said unto the king, If it please the king, let letters be given me to the governors beyond the river, that they may convey me over till I come into Judah;

Neh 2:8 And a letter unto Asaph the keeper of the king's forest, that he may give me timber to make beams for the gates of the palace which appertained to the house, and for the wall of the city, and for the house that I shall enter into. And the king granted me, according to the good hand of my God upon me.

Nehemiah 2:2-8

Even Jesus had stewards in his life. They helped meet the needs of his ministry. This was the case when he wanted to have the Passover.

The disciples wanted to know where he wanted to have it. By the supply of God, he knew a steward who had such a hosting facility. He asked for it and received it to celebrate the Passover:

Mat 26:17 Now the first day of the feast of unleavened bread the disciples came to Jesus, saying unto him, Where wilt thou that we prepare for thee to eat the passover?

Mat 26:18 And he said, Go into the city to such a man, and say unto him, The Master saith, My time is at hand; I will keep the passover at thy house with my disciples.

Mat 26:19 And the disciples did as Jesus had appointed them; and they made ready the passover.

Matthew 26:17-19

Let this revelation guide you.

You must locate your stewards and ask them for their help in meeting your needs, it is biblical and there is nothing evil about it.

God clearly instructed us to:

Mat 7:7 Ask, and it shall be given you; seek, and ye shall find; knock, and it shall be opened unto you:

Matthew 7:7

Many people have missed out on the supply of God because they were too shy or proud to ask stewards for supply to their needs.

God wants you to ask. There is nothing shameful about it.

Though we reject fellowship with Jesus all the time, he still knocks at the door of our hearts. Have a change of mind and you can enjoy the supply of God through stewards.

Rev 3:20 Behold, I stand at the door, and knock: if any man hear my voice, and open the door, I will come in to him, and will sup with him, and he with me.

Revelation 3:20

This is the time to identify your stewards and ask for the required supply. Be bold about it. And in the unlikely case of rejection, just know that you just have to identify the right steward to receive the supply of God.

That supply is available.

In the next chapter, I share some important words.

CHAPTER NINE

DON'T LIMIT YOURSELF

Many people have limited themselves to only prayer to receive the supply of God. This should not be you from henceforth.

You have the unique opportunity to use any of the mechanisms by which God supplies our needs.

If you diligently pursue the means God has made available for His children to have their needs met, you will come back celebrating the goodness of God.

Please get my book "[Provision Through Divine Ideas](#)". It will bless you greatly.

My desire is to see your progress and prosperity and freedom from negative people and circumstances. Because of that, please permit me to introduce two courses that I believe passionately will help you.

1. To cure prayerlessness, an inconsistent prayer life and the pain of not enjoying all that God has made available to you,, click here to learn more about my 3 Day Course on "How to Overcome prayerlessness" that will solve the problem of prayerlessness in your life.

2.To overcome the pain of not having enough money to live where you want, eat what you want to eat and be a blessing to the multitudes around you, I have created a 7 Day Financial Abundance Course that will deliver financial abundance to you quickly.

Click here to learn more about that course.

REVIEW

Because your review is important to help others benefit from these books, please leave a good review [here](#)

Please check out my other books on the next page

Printed in Great Britain
by Amazon